MW00953118

THE ULTIMATE GUIDE TO

BUYING AND SELLING

AMAZON RETURN PALLETS

Unlock Profit Potential, Master Sourcing and Sorting, Implement Effective Selling Tactics, and Achieve Business Success as a Reseller or Entrepreneur

MILLY HARPER

Welcome Message

Dear Reader,

Welcome to "The Ultimate Guide to Buying and Selling Amazon Return Pallets." I'm thrilled to embark on this journey with you as we delve into the exciting world of reselling and explore the lucrative opportunities offered by Amazon return pallets.

In this comprehensive guide, we'll navigate through the intricacies of sourcing, sorting, and selling Amazon return pallets, uncovering valuable insights and strategies to help you maximize profits and achieve success in the reselling industry. Whether you're a seasoned reseller looking to expand your business or a newcomer eager to explore the possibilities of reselling, this book is designed to provide you with the knowledge, tools, and inspiration needed to thrive in this dynamic marketplace.

Get ready to unlock your reselling potential, master the art of buying and selling Amazon return pallets, and embark on a rewarding journey towards financial independence and entrepreneurial success.

Thank you for joining me on this adventure. Let's dive in and begin our exploration of "The Ultimate Guide to Buying and Selling Amazon Return Pallets"!

Warm regards,

[MILLY HARPER]

CONTENTS

ABOUT THE AUTHOR

MILLY HARPER is a seasoned entrepreneur and reselling expert with 10 years of experience in the e-commerce industry. With a passion for entrepreneurship and a keen eye for opportunity, MILLY HARPER has successfully built and scaled multiple reselling businesses, specializing in the profitable niche of Amazon return pallets.

Throughout MILLY HAPER's career, they have developed a deep understanding of the reselling landscape, honing their skills in sourcing, sorting, and selling various types of merchandise, including electronics, apparel, home goods, and more. Their expertise in navigating online marketplaces, negotiating with suppliers, and implementing effective sales strategies has earned them recognition as a trusted authority in the reselling community.

As a dedicated mentor and educator, MILLY HARPER is committed to sharing their knowledge and insights with aspiring resellers, helping them unlock their full potential and achieve success in the competitive world of e-commerce. Through "The

Ultimate Guide to Buying and Selling Amazon Return Pallets," MILLY HARPER aims to empower readers with practical guidance, actionable advice, and proven strategies for building profitable reselling businesses with Amazon return pallets.

When not immersed in the world of reselling, MILLY HARPER enjoys spending time with family, traveling, and exploring new business opportunities.

INTRODUCTION

Why Amazon Return Pallets?

Amazon return pallets have emerged as a compelling opportunity for resellers looking to capitalize on the vast inventory of returned merchandise from one of the world's largest online retailers. But why choose Amazon return pallets over other sourcing options?

1. **Diverse Product Selection:** Amazon return pallets contain a wide range of products spanning various categories, including electronics, apparel, home goods, toys, and more. This diversity allows resellers to cater to different markets and meet the evolving needs of their customers.

2. **Cost-Effective Sourcing:** Amazon return pallets are typically sold at discounted prices, making them a cost-effective option for resellers looking to acquire inventory at wholesale rates. With the potential for high-profit margins,

reselling Amazon return pallets offers a lucrative opportunity for entrepreneurs seeking to maximize their returns on investment.

3. **Scalability and Flexibility:** Whether you're a part-time reseller operating from home or a full-fledged e-commerce business looking to scale operations, Amazon return pallets offer scalability and flexibility to accommodate your business needs. With the ability to purchase pallets in bulk or smaller quantities, resellers can tailor their inventory management strategies to suit their growth objectives.

4. **Sustainability and Environmental Impact:** By reselling Amazon return pallets, resellers contribute to the circular economy by giving returned products a second chance at finding new homes. This sustainable approach to commerce not only reduces waste but also minimizes the environmental impact of excess inventory.

5. **Opportunity for Innovation:** Reselling Amazon return pallets presents an opportunity for innovation and creativity in the reselling space. With the ability to uncover hidden gems, bundle complementary products, and experiment with different sales channels, resellers can explore new avenues for revenue generation and business growth.

In the following chapters of "Resell Mastery," we'll delve deeper into the strategies, techniques, and best practices for effectively buying and selling Amazon return pallets. Get ready to unlock the full potential of this exciting reselling opportunity and embark on a journey towards entrepreneurial success!

CHAPTER 1

Understanding Amazon Return Pallets

Amazon return pallets have revolutionized the world of reselling, offering entrepreneurs and businesses alike an opportunity to tap into a vast inventory of returned merchandise from one of the world's largest online retailers. In this chapter, we'll delve deep into the intricacies of Amazon return pallets, exploring what they are, why they're attractive to resellers, and what you can expect to find within them.

1.1 Definition and Overview

Amazon return pallets, also known as liquidation pallets or customer return pallets, are bundles of merchandise that have been returned by customers to Amazon for various reasons. These pallets typically contain a mix of items, ranging from electronics and appliances to apparel, home goods, toys, and more.

One of the key characteristics of Amazon return pallets is their diversity. Unlike traditional wholesale lots that may focus on specific categories or types of products, return pallets offer a wide range of merchandise, making them appealing to resellers looking for variety in their inventory.

1.2 The Appeal of Amazon Return Pallets

So, what makes Amazon return pallets such an attractive option for resellers? There are several factors at play:

- **Cost-Effectiveness:**

Amazon return pallets are often sold at significantly discounted prices compared to their retail value. This presents an opportunity for resellers to acquire inventory at a fraction of the cost, allowing them to maximize their profit margins when reselling the items.

- **Scalability:**

Whether you're just starting out as a part-time reseller or running a full-fledged e-commerce business, Amazon return pallets offer scalability to accommodate your business needs. You can choose to purchase pallets in bulk or smaller quantities, depending on your budget and storage capacity.

- **Potential for High-Profit Margins:**

Due to the discounted nature of return pallets, resellers have the potential to achieve high-profit margins on their sales. By effectively sorting through the merchandise and identifying valuable items, resellers can capitalize on hidden gems and premium products within the pallets.

- **Sustainability:**

Reselling Amazon return pallets contributes to a more sustainable approach to commerce by giving returned products a second chance at finding new homes. This circular economy model helps reduce waste and minimize the environmental impact of excess inventory.

1.3 The Journey of Unsold Products

When products are returned to Amazon but don't end up back on the virtual shelves, they enter the realm of unsold merchandise. This can happen for various reasons, including customer dissatisfaction, shipping damage, or simply being overstocked. Instead of being discarded or destroyed, these products are aggregated into return pallets for resale.

Understanding the journey of unsold products is crucial for resellers, as it sheds light on the types of items they can expect to find within Amazon return pallets. From brand-new, unopened items to slightly used or damaged goods, return pallets can contain a mix of merchandise in varying conditions.

1.4 Contents of Amazon Return Pallets

The contents of Amazon return pallets can vary widely, depending on factors such as the category, seasonality, and reason for return. However, common items found within return pallets include:

- **Electronics:** This category may include items such as smartphones, tablets, laptops, gaming consoles, and accessories.

- **Apparel:** Clothing, shoes, and accessories are frequently found in return pallets, ranging from brand-name apparel to generic brands.

- **Home Goods:** Kitchen appliances, home decor, bedding, and furniture are often included in return pallets.

- **Toys and Games:** Children's toys, games, puzzles, and other recreational items can be found within return pallets.

- **Health and Beauty:** Cosmetics, skincare products, grooming tools, and supplements may be part of the pallet contents.

It's important for resellers to carefully inspect and evaluate the contents of each pallet to determine its potential value and profitability.

CHAPTER 2

Sourcing Strategies

In Chapter 1, we explored the fundamentals of Amazon return pallets, understanding their appeal and the contents they typically contain. Now, let's delve into the crucial aspect of sourcing strategies. Sourcing the right pallets is essential for resellers to acquire quality inventory at competitive prices and maximize their profitability. In this chapter, we'll discuss various sourcing strategies, from finding reliable suppliers to navigating online platforms and local auctions.

2.1 Finding Reliable Suppliers

The foundation of successful pallet sourcing lies in establishing relationships with reliable suppliers. These suppliers play a crucial role in providing access to quality inventory and ensuring a smooth transaction process.

Here are some strategies for finding and vetting suppliers:

- **Direct Relationships:**

Building direct relationships with wholesalers, liquidators, and pallet brokers can offer several advantages, including access to exclusive deals and personalized service. Attend trade shows, industry events, and networking meetings to connect with potential suppliers and establish mutually beneficial partnerships.

- **Online Directories:**

Utilize online directories and platforms that specialize in connecting resellers with wholesale suppliers. Websites such as Liquidation.com, B-Stock, and Direct Liquidation provide a comprehensive list of verified suppliers offering a wide range of pallets.

- **Referrals and Recommendations:**

Seek recommendations from fellow resellers, industry experts, and online communities. Referrals from trusted sources can help you identify reputable suppliers and avoid potential scams or fraudulent operations.

- **Background Research:**

Conduct thorough research on prospective suppliers, including verifying their credentials, reviewing customer testimonials and reviews, and assessing their track record in the industry. Look for suppliers with a proven reputation for reliability, transparency, and integrity.

2.2 Online Platforms for Purchasing

The internet has revolutionized the way resellers source inventory, offering access to a plethora of online platforms and marketplaces.

Here are some popular online platforms for purchasing Amazon return pallets:

THE ULTIMATE GUIDE TO BUYING AND SELLING AMAZON RETURN PALLETS

- **Marketplace Websites:**

Online marketplaces such as eBay, Amazon Warehouse Deals, and Craigslist often feature listings for Amazon return pallets from individual sellers and liquidation companies. These platforms allow resellers to browse through a variety of listings, compare prices, and place bids or make purchases directly.

- **Wholesale Auction Sites:**

Auction-based websites like B-Stock and Liquidation.com specialize in connecting resellers with liquidation auctions from major retailers, including Amazon. These platforms offer a wide selection of pallets in various categories, allowing resellers to bid on inventory and secure deals at competitive prices.

23 | P a g e

- ## Specialized Liquidators:

Some liquidation companies specialize in sourcing and selling Amazon return pallets exclusively. These companies often have direct partnerships with Amazon and other retailers, providing access to premium inventory and exclusive deals. Examples include Via Trading, Merchandize Liquidators, and 888 Lots.

2.3 Local Auctions and Liquidation Centers

In addition to online platforms, resellers can explore local auctions and liquidation centers as alternative sourcing channels. Here's how to leverage these opportunities effectively:

- ## Auction Houses:

Attend local auctions hosted by auction houses, storage facilities, or bankruptcy courts to bid on pallets of returned merchandise. These auctions may offer a diverse range of inventory at discounted prices, allowing resellers to acquire pallets through competitive bidding.

- **Liquidation Centers:**

Visit local liquidation centers or warehouse outlets that specialize in selling pallets of returned and surplus merchandise. These centers may offer discounted prices on pallets that are available for immediate purchase, providing resellers with the opportunity to inspect the inventory firsthand and negotiate deals in person.

- **Networking Events:**

Participate in networking events, industry conferences, and trade shows in your area to connect with local suppliers, wholesalers, and fellow resellers. These events offer opportunities to build relationships, exchange information, and discover new sourcing channels within your community.

2.4 Negotiation Techniques

Once you've identified potential suppliers and sourcing channels, mastering negotiation techniques is essential for securing the best deals and maximizing your profitability. Effective negotiation can help you achieve favorable pricing, favorable terms, and build strong relationships with your suppliers.

Here are some key negotiation techniques to consider:

- **Understand Your Value Proposition**:
  Before entering into negotiations, it's crucial to understand your value proposition as a reseller. Highlight your strengths, such as your purchasing volume, market knowledge, and ability to move inventory quickly. Emphasize the value you bring to the table and how working with you can benefit the supplier.

- **Research and Preparation**:

Conduct thorough research on the market value of the products you're interested in and the typical pricing for similar pallets. Armed with this knowledge, you'll be better equipped to negotiate effectively and avoid overpaying for inventory. Additionally, gather information about the supplier's pricing structure, terms, and any potential discounts or incentives they may offer.

- **Establish Clear Objectives:**

Define your negotiation objectives upfront and prioritize your goals. Whether you're aiming for lower prices, favorable payment terms, or additional perks such as free shipping or extended warranties, clarity on your objectives will guide your negotiation strategy and help you stay focused during discussions.

- **Build Rapport and Trust:**

Establishing rapport and building trust with your supplier is essential for fostering a positive negotiation environment. Take the time to listen actively, ask questions, and show genuine interest in their business. Demonstrating professionalism, integrity, and reliability can go a long way in building a mutually beneficial relationship based on trust and respect.

- **Seek Win-Win Solutions:**

Aim for win-win outcomes where both parties benefit from the negotiation. Look for creative solutions that address the needs and concerns of both you and the supplier. By focusing on mutual gains and fostering collaboration, you can build long-term partnerships that are sustainable and mutually rewarding.

- **Be Flexible and Adaptive:**

Flexibility is key in negotiation, as circumstances may change, and unexpected challenges may arise. Be prepared to adapt your negotiation strategy as needed and explore alternative options to overcome obstacles and reach a satisfactory agreement. Maintain a positive attitude and approach negotiations with a willingness to compromise when necessary.

- **Follow Up and Follow Through:**

Once an agreement has been reached, it's important to follow up promptly and ensure that all terms and conditions are clearly documented and understood by both parties. Follow through on your commitments, meet deadlines, and communicate openly and transparently to build trust and credibility with your supplier.

CHAPTER 3

Sorting and Evaluation

Once you've acquired Amazon return pallets, the next crucial step is sorting through the merchandise and evaluating the condition of the items. Effective sorting and evaluation techniques are essential for identifying high-value items, assessing potential profitability, and ensuring customer satisfaction. In this section, we'll explore strategies for streamlining the sorting process and maximizing the value of your inventory.

3.3.1 Efficient Sorting Strategies

Sorting through Amazon return pallets requires a systematic approach to ensure that you maximize efficiency and accuracy.

Here are some efficient sorting strategies to streamline the process:

- **Prioritize Categories:**

Start by categorizing the items into broad product categories such as electronics, apparel, home goods, toys, and miscellaneous. This initial sorting will give you a clear overview of the contents of the pallet and help you identify any standout items.

- **Use Sorting Tools:**

Invest in sorting tools such as bins, shelves, and labeling systems to keep the process organized. Designate specific areas for each product category to prevent clutter and confusion. Having a designated workspace with adequate lighting and ventilation can also enhance productivity.

- **Implement a Systematic Approach:**

Develop a systematic approach to sorting, such as sorting by product type, brand, or condition. Create a checklist or workflow to guide you through the sorting process and ensure that no items are overlooked. Consistency is key to maintaining efficiency and accuracy.

- **Work in Batches:**

Break down the sorting process into manageable batches to prevent overwhelm and maintain focus. Set realistic goals for each sorting session and take breaks as needed to avoid fatigue. By pacing yourself and working systematically, you can avoid burnout and maintain productivity throughout the sorting process.

- **Utilize Technology:**

Consider leveraging technology to streamline the sorting process. Barcode scanners, inventory management software, and product identification tools can help expedite the sorting process and minimize errors. These tools can also provide valuable data insights that can inform your decision-making process.

- **Collaborate with Team Members:**

If you have a team of employees or collaborators, consider dividing the sorting tasks among team members to expedite the process. Assign specific roles and responsibilities based on each team member's strengths and expertise. Effective communication and collaboration are essential for maximizing efficiency and ensuring a smooth sorting process.

- **Continuous Improvement:**

Regularly evaluate and refine your sorting process to identify areas for improvement. Solicit feedback from team members and stakeholders to gather insights and perspectives on how to optimize the process further. By continuously striving for improvement, you can enhance efficiency, productivity, and overall effectiveness in sorting Amazon return pallets.

By implementing these efficient sorting strategies, you can streamline the sorting process, minimize errors, and maximize the value of your inventory from Amazon return pallets.

3.3.2 Evaluating Product Condition

Once you've sorted the merchandise into categories, it's time to evaluate the condition of each item to determine its resale potential. Here are some factors to consider when assessing product condition:

- **Visual Inspection:**

Conduct a visual inspection of each item to identify any visible signs of damage, wear, or defects. Look for scratches, dents, missing parts, or other issues that may affect the item's value or usability.

- **Functional Testing:**

Test electronic items, appliances, and other products that require power or functionality to ensure they are in working order. Use appropriate testing equipment and follow manufacturer guidelines for testing procedures.

- ## Refer to Product Descriptions:

Review product descriptions and specifications provided by the manufacturer or retailer to understand the expected condition and features of the item. Compare the actual condition of the item to the description to determine if it meets expectations.

- ## Check for Documentation:

Look for original packaging, manuals, warranty cards, and other documentation that may accompany the item. Complete sets with documentation may command a higher resale value than items without documentation.

3.3.3 Identifying High-Value Items

As you sort through the merchandise and evaluate product condition, keep an eye out for high-value items that have the potential to generate significant profits. Here are some indicators of high-value items:

- **Brand Recognition:**

Items from well-known brands or popular manufacturers often command higher resale prices due to consumer trust and brand loyalty.

- **Rare or Limited Edition:**

Rare or limited-edition items with unique features, designs, or collectible appeal can fetch premium prices among collectors and enthusiasts.

- **High Demand:**

Products that are in high demand or trending in the market may sell quickly and at higher prices. Stay informed about current trends and consumer preferences to capitalize on demand-driven opportunities.

- **Condition and Quality:**

Items in excellent condition, with minimal signs of wear or damage, typically command higher resale prices than items in poor condition. Focus on sourcing high-quality merchandise with the potential for resale.

By implementing efficient sorting strategies, thorough product evaluation techniques, and a keen eye for high-value items, you can optimize the value of your inventory and maximize profits in your reselling business.

CHAPTER 4

Sales and Marketing Tactics

In Chapter 4 of "The Ultimate Guide to Buying and Selling Amazon Return Pallets," we'll explore various sales and marketing tactics to help you effectively sell the inventory acquired from Amazon return pallets. From selecting the right sales channels to implementing pricing strategies and providing exceptional customer service, this chapter will equip you with the tools and techniques needed to maximize your profits and reach a wider audience.

4.1 Choosing the Right Sales Channels

Selecting the right sales channels is crucial for reaching your target audience and maximizing your sales potential.

Here's an in-depth exploration of various sales channels to consider:

- ## Online Marketplaces:

Online marketplaces like Amazon, eBay, and Etsy offer a vast reach and built-in customer base, making them ideal platforms for selling a wide range of products from Amazon return pallets. Each marketplace has its own set of rules, fees, and seller tools, so it's essential to research and understand the requirements of each platform before listing your products. Consider factors such as seller fees, shipping options, and customer service support when choosing which marketplaces to sell on.

- ## E-commerce Website:

Launching your own e-commerce website gives you full control over your brand and customer experience. Platforms like Shopify, WooCommerce, and BigCommerce provide user-friendly tools for building and managing your online store. When setting up your e-commerce website, focus on creating a seamless shopping experience for your customers, with easy navigation, clear product descriptions, and secure payment options. Invest in search engine optimization (SEO) to improve your website's visibility in search engine results and drive organic traffic to your store.

- ## Social Media Platforms:

Social media platforms such as Facebook, Instagram, and Pinterest offer valuable opportunities for promoting your products and engaging with your audience. Create business profiles on these platforms and regularly share compelling content, such as product photos, behind-the-scenes videos, and customer testimonials. Use targeted advertising to reach potential customers based on their demographics, interests, and online behavior. Engage with your followers by responding to comments, answering questions, and participating in relevant conversations.

- ## Local Markets and Events:

Selling your products at local markets, craft fairs, and community events allows you to connect directly with customers and showcase your products in person. Research local markets and events in your area and apply to become a vendor. When participating in local markets, focus on creating an attractive display that showcases your products effectively and attracts passersby. Offer special promotions or discounts to incentivize purchases and encourage repeat business.

By carefully evaluating each sales channel and choosing the ones that align with your business goals and target audience, you can maximize your reach and increase your sales potential.

4.2 Pricing Strategies for Maximizing Profits

Pricing your products effectively is essential for maximizing profits and staying competitive in the reselling market. Here's a comprehensive look at pricing strategies to consider:

- **Competitive Pricing:**

Research competitor prices and market trends to ensure your prices are competitive while still allowing for a healthy profit margin. Analyze pricing data from similar products on online marketplaces, e-commerce websites, and other sales channels to determine the optimal price range for your products. Keep in mind factors such as product condition, brand reputation, and customer demand when setting your prices.

- **Dynamic Pricing:**

Implement dynamic pricing strategies that adjust prices based on factors such as demand, seasonality, and competitor prices. Dynamic pricing software can automatically adjust your prices in real-time based on market conditions, inventory levels, and other variables. This flexibility allows you to optimize your prices for maximum profitability and respond quickly to changes in the market.

- **Bundle Pricing:**

Bundle complementary products together and offer them at a discounted price to encourage upsells and increase average order value. Bundle pricing can help you move slow-selling items, promote related products, and attract customers looking for value-added deals. Experiment with different bundle combinations and pricing structures to find the optimal mix for your target audience.

- ## Discount Pricing:

Offer discounts and promotions to attract customers and stimulate sales. Consider running limited-time promotions, flash sales, or clearance events to create a sense of urgency and encourage impulse purchases. Use pricing psychology techniques such as price anchoring, scarcity, and social proof to influence purchasing behavior and drive sales.

- ## Value-Based Pricing:

Set prices based on the perceived value of your products rather than the cost of goods sold. Focus on highlighting the unique features, benefits, and value propositions of your products to justify higher prices. Use persuasive language, storytelling, and customer testimonials to convey the value proposition and justify premium pricing.

- **Monitor and Adjust Prices:**

Regularly monitor your pricing strategy and adjust prices as needed to stay competitive and maximize profitability. Use sales data, customer feedback, and market insights to inform your pricing decisions and identify opportunities for optimization. Be flexible and responsive to changes in the market, customer preferences, and competitive landscape.

By implementing these pricing strategies and continuously monitoring and adjusting your prices, you can optimize your pricing strategy for maximum profitability and sales growth.

4.3 Customer Service and Returns Handling

Providing exceptional customer service is essential for building trust, loyalty, and repeat business.

In this section, we'll explore strategies for delivering outstanding customer service and handling returns effectively:

- **Prompt Communication:**

Respond to customer inquiries, messages, and feedback promptly and professionally. Aim to provide timely and helpful responses to address customer questions, resolve issues, and address concerns. Use multiple communication channels such as email, phone, and social media to make it easy for customers to reach you.

- **Fast Shipping:**

Ship orders quickly and accurately to ensure a positive customer experience. Set clear expectations for shipping times and delivery estimates, and provide tracking information to keep customers informed about the status of their orders. Invest in reliable shipping carriers and packaging materials to minimize shipping delays and damage.

• Easy Returns and Refunds:

Make the returns and refunds process as seamless as possible for customers to encourage trust and repeat business. Clearly communicate your return policy, including timeframes, eligibility criteria, and procedures for returning products. Offer hassle-free returns and refunds, and be flexible in accommodating customer requests.

• Personalized Service:

Provide personalized service to each customer to make them feel valued and appreciated. Use customer data and purchase history to personalize communications, recommend products, and offer tailored promotions. Address customers by name, thank them for their business, and go above and beyond to exceed their expectations.

- **Proactive Problem-Solving:**

Anticipate and proactively address potential issues or concerns before they escalate into larger problems. Monitor customer feedback, reviews, and social media mentions to identify areas for improvement and take corrective action as needed. Use customer feedback to inform product improvements, service enhancements, and process optimizations.

- **Continuous Improvement:**

Regularly evaluate and improve your customer service processes and procedures to enhance the overall customer experience. Solicit feedback from customers, gather insights from customer service interactions, and implement changes based on lessons learned and best practices. Continuously strive to exceed customer expectations and deliver exceptional service at every touchpoint.

By prioritizing customer service excellence and adopting a customer-centric approach, you can build strong relationships with your customers, foster loyalty, and differentiate your reselling business from competitors.

4.4 Marketing Your Reselling Business

Marketing plays a crucial role in promoting your reselling business and attracting customers.

In this section, we'll explore various marketing strategies and tactics to help you reach your target audience and drive sales:

- **Search Engine Optimization (SEO):**

Optimize your product listings and website content for search engines to improve visibility and attract organic traffic. Conduct keyword research to identify relevant search terms and incorporate them into your product titles, descriptions, and metadata. Focus on creating high-quality, informative content that provides value to your audience and positions you as an authority in your niche.

- ## Email Marketing:

Build an email list of past customers and prospects and use email marketing to stay in touch with them on a regular basis. Send out newsletters, promotions, and product updates to keep subscribers engaged and informed about your latest offerings. Segment your email list based on customer preferences, purchase history, and behavior to deliver targeted, personalized messages that resonate with your audience.

- ## Social Media Marketing:

Utilize social media platforms such as Facebook, Instagram, and Twitter to connect with your audience, showcase your products, and drive traffic to your website or online store. Create engaging content, including product photos, videos, tutorials, and behind-the-scenes glimpses, to attract followers and encourage them to interact with your brand. Use social media advertising to reach new audiences and promote your products to targeted demographics.

- ## Content Marketing:

Create valuable, informative content that educates, entertains, and inspires your audience. Publish blog posts, articles, guides, and tutorials that address common questions, provide solutions to problems, and offer insights into your industry. Share your content on your website, social media channels, and email newsletters to attract inbound traffic, establish credibility, and build trust with your audience.

- ## Influencer Marketing:

Partner with influencers, bloggers, and content creators in your niche to promote your products to their followers. Identify influencers who align with your brand values and target audience, and collaborate with them on sponsored content, product reviews, and endorsements. Leverage their reach and influence to increase brand awareness, drive traffic, and generate sales.

- **Paid Advertising:**

Invest in paid advertising channels such as Google Ads, Facebook Ads, and sponsored content to reach potential customers and drive targeted traffic to your website or product listings. Set clear goals and objectives for your ad campaigns, and monitor performance metrics such as click-through rates, conversion rates, and return on investment (ROI) to optimize your campaigns for maximum results.

By implementing these marketing strategies and tactics, you can increase brand awareness, attract new customers, and drive sales for your reselling business.

4.5 Customer Retention Strategies

While attracting new customers is important, retaining existing customers is equally crucial for the long-term success of your reselling business.

In this section, we'll explore effective customer retention strategies:

1. **Provide Excellent Customer Service:** Continuously strive to exceed customer expectations by providing excellent customer service. Be responsive to customer inquiries, address any issues or concerns promptly, and go the extra mile to ensure customer satisfaction. Happy customers are more likely to become repeat customers and recommend your business to others.

2. **Offer Loyalty Rewards:** Implement a loyalty rewards program to incentivize repeat purchases and encourage customer loyalty. Offer discounts, exclusive offers, or freebies to customers who make multiple purchases or refer

others to your business. A loyalty program can help you retain customers and increase their lifetime value to your business.

3. **Personalize the Shopping Experience:** Use customer data and purchase history to personalize the shopping experience for each customer. Recommend products based on their past purchases, send personalized offers and promotions, and address them by name in communications. Personalization helps create a more engaging and relevant shopping experience, which can lead to increased customer loyalty.

4. **Stay in Touch:** Stay in touch with your customers through regular communication channels such as email newsletters, social media updates, and promotional campaigns. Keep them informed about new products, special offers, and company news to maintain top-of-mind awareness and encourage repeat purchases.

5. Gather Feedback and Act on It: Regularly solicit feedback from your customers through surveys, reviews, and social media interactions. Use this feedback to identify areas for improvement and make necessary changes to enhance the customer experience. Show customers that their opinions matter and that you are committed to providing the best possible service.

6. Build a Community Around Your Brand: Create a sense of community around your brand by engaging with customers on social media, hosting events or contests, and encouraging user-generated content. A strong community can foster loyalty among customers and turn them into brand advocates who promote your business to others.

7. Offer Exceptional Value: Provide exceptional value to your customers through high-quality products, competitive prices, and outstanding customer service. Make sure that every interaction with your brand leaves a positive impression and reinforces the value proposition of your products and services.

By implementing these customer retention strategies, you can build long-lasting relationships with your customers, increase their loyalty to your brand, and drive repeat business.

CHAPTER 5

Inventory Management and Business Operations

5.1 Inventory Tracking and Management

Efficient inventory tracking and management are essential for running a successful reselling business.

In this section, we'll explore strategies for effectively managing your inventory:

- **Inventory Tracking Systems:**

Implement inventory tracking systems to monitor stock levels, track sales, and identify fast-moving and slow-moving items. Choose a system that aligns with your business needs and allows for real-time inventory visibility across multiple sales channels.

- **Stock Replenishment Strategies:**

Develop stock replenishment strategies to ensure that you always have enough inventory on hand to meet customer demand. Use historical sales data, seasonal trends, and sales forecasts to anticipate future demand and reorder stock accordingly.

- **Just-In-Time Inventory Management:**

Consider adopting a just-in-time (JIT) inventory management approach to minimize storage costs and reduce excess inventory. With JIT inventory management, you only order and receive inventory as needed, helping you maintain leaner inventory levels and optimize cash flow.

- **Batch and Lot Tracking:**

Implement batch and lot tracking systems to trace the origin and movement of products throughout the supply chain. This allows you to track product recalls, monitor expiration dates, and ensure compliance with regulatory requirements.

- ## Cycle Counting and Auditing

Conduct regular cycle counting and auditing to verify the accuracy of your inventory records and identify any discrepancies. Develop a schedule for ongoing inventory counts and audits to maintain data integrity and minimize errors.

- ## Warehouse Organization and Layout:

Optimize your warehouse layout and organization to maximize storage space and improve operational efficiency. Use shelving, racks, and labeling systems to categorize and store inventory items systematically, making it easy to locate and retrieve products when needed.

- ## Inventory Analysis and Optimization:

Regularly analyze your inventory data to identify trends, assess product performance, and optimize your inventory mix. Identify slow-moving items and implement strategies to clear excess inventory, such as markdowns, promotions, or bundle deals.

By implementing these inventory tracking and management strategies, you can ensure that your reselling business operates smoothly and efficiently, with optimized inventory levels and minimized costs.

5.2 Building a Network of Buyers and Suppliers

Establishing strong relationships with buyers and suppliers is crucial for sourcing quality inventory and maximizing sales opportunities.

In this section, we'll explore strategies for building and nurturing your network of buyers and suppliers:

- **Identifying Potential Buyers and Suppliers:**

Research potential buyers and suppliers in your industry by attending trade shows, networking events, and industry conferences. Use online platforms such as LinkedIn, industry forums, and supplier directories to identify and connect with potential partners.

- **Building Relationships**

Invest time and effort into building meaningful relationships with buyers and suppliers based on trust, transparency, and mutual respect. Communicate openly, listen attentively, and follow through on commitments to demonstrate your reliability and commitment to the partnership.

- **Negotiating Terms and Agreements:**

Negotiate favorable terms and agreements with buyers and suppliers to ensure mutually beneficial partnerships. Discuss pricing, payment terms, delivery schedules, and quality standards to align expectations and minimize misunderstandings.

- **Maintaining Communication:**

Maintain regular communication with buyers and suppliers to stay informed about market trends, product availability, and changing customer preferences. Keep them updated about your inventory needs, sales goals, and any relevant changes to your business operations.

- **Offering Value-Added Services:**

Offer value-added services to differentiate yourself from competitors and provide additional value to your buyers and suppliers. This could include offering personalized product recommendations, providing marketing support, or offering flexible payment options.

- **Resolving Disputes and Issues:**

Handle disputes and issues with buyers and suppliers promptly and professionally to maintain positive relationships. Listen to their concerns, seek mutually acceptable solutions, and follow up to ensure that any issues are resolved to their satisfaction.

- ## Expanding Your Network:

Continuously expand your network of buyers and suppliers by actively seeking out new opportunities and exploring potential partnerships. Attend industry events, join professional associations, and leverage online platforms to connect with new contacts and grow your network.

By building and nurturing relationships with buyers and suppliers, you can create a reliable and sustainable network that supports your reselling business's growth and success.

5.3 Staying Updated with Industry Trends

Staying informed about industry trends is essential for maintaining a competitive edge and adapting to changing market conditions.

In this section, we'll explore strategies for staying updated with industry trends:

- **Market Research:**

Conduct regular market research to stay informed about industry trends, consumer preferences, and competitive landscape. Monitor industry publications, market reports, and news sources to gather insights and identify emerging trends.

- **Networking and Collaboration:**

Network with industry peers, attend industry events, and participate in online forums and communities to stay connected with industry trends. Collaborate with other resellers, suppliers, and industry professionals to exchange ideas and share knowledge.

- **Customer Feedback and Insights:**

Gather feedback from your customers through surveys, reviews, and social media interactions to understand their preferences and behaviors. Use this information to tailor your product offerings and marketing strategies to better meet their needs.

- **Technology and Innovation:**

Stay abreast of technological advancements and innovations in your industry that could impact your business. Explore new technologies, tools, and platforms that can help you streamline your operations, improve efficiency, and enhance the customer experience.

- **Industry Events and Conferences:**

Attend industry events, trade shows, and conferences to stay updated with the latest trends and developments. Engage with industry experts, attend seminars and workshops, and participate in panel discussions to gain valuable insights and perspectives.

- **Continuous Learning:**

Commit to continuous learning and professional development to stay ahead of industry trends. Take courses, read books, and participate in webinars and training programs to expand your knowledge and skills in reselling and business management.

- **Adaptation and Flexibility:**

Be prepared to adapt to changing market conditions and trends by being flexible and agile in your business approach. Monitor key performance indicators (KPIs) and adjust your strategies and tactics accordingly to stay competitive and profitable.

By staying updated with industry trends and embracing innovation, you can position your reselling business for long-term success and growth in a dynamic and ever-changing market.

5.4 Legal and Compliance Considerations

Ensuring compliance with legal requirements and regulations is essential for protecting your reselling business and maintaining trust with customers and suppliers.

In this section, we'll explore key legal and compliance considerations:

- **Business Registration and Licensing:**

Ensure that you understand the legal requirements for registering your reselling business in your jurisdiction. Depending on your location and business structure, you may need to register your business with the state or local government, obtain a business license, and register for a sales tax permit. Research the specific requirements applicable to your business and ensure that you comply with all necessary regulations to operate legally.

- **Tax Obligations:**

Consult with a qualified tax professional to understand your tax obligations as a reseller. This includes collecting and remitting sales tax on applicable sales, reporting business income accurately on your tax returns, and paying any other business taxes required by law. Keep detailed records of your sales, expenses, and tax filings to ensure compliance with tax regulations and minimize the risk of audits or penalties.

- **Product Compliance:**

Verify that the products you resell comply with all relevant safety standards, regulations, and certifications. This may include product testing, certification by accredited laboratories, and compliance with labeling and packaging requirements. Stay informed about any updates or changes to product regulations in your industry and ensure that your inventory meets all legal requirements to protect your customers and your business.

- **Intellectual Property Rights:**

Educate yourself about intellectual property laws and take steps to avoid infringing on the intellectual property rights of others. Research trademarks, copyrights, and patents related to the products you sell to ensure that you are not violating any protected rights. Be cautious when using brand names, logos, or copyrighted materials in your marketing materials or product listings, and obtain permission or licensing when necessary to avoid legal disputes.

- **Consumer Protection Laws:**

Understand the consumer protection laws that apply to your business, including laws governing advertising, product warranties, and consumer rights. Ensure that your marketing materials and product descriptions are accurate and not deceptive, and honor any warranties or guarantees offered to customers. Comply with regulations regarding online sales, such as providing clear information about pricing, shipping costs, and return policies to consumers.

- **Data Privacy and Security:**

Protect the privacy and security of customer data collected through your website or online store by implementing appropriate data protection measures. This may include encrypting sensitive information, restricting access to customer data, and implementing secure payment processing systems. Comply with data privacy laws and regulations applicable to your business, such as the GDPR in the European Union or the California Consumer Privacy Act (CCPA) in the United States, to safeguard customer information and avoid legal penalties.

- **Contracts and Agreements:**

Use written contracts and agreements to formalize business relationships with buyers, suppliers, and partners. Clearly outline the terms and conditions of the agreement, including pricing, payment terms, delivery obligations, and dispute resolution mechanisms. Consult with legal professionals to draft contracts that protect your interests and mitigate risks, and ensure that all parties involved understand and agree to the terms before entering into any agreements.

By taking a proactive approach to legal and compliance considerations, you can protect your reselling business from legal risks, build trust with customers and suppliers, and ensure long-term success in the marketplace.

CHAPTER 6:

Case Studies and Success Stories

6.1 Real-Life Examples of Successful Resellers

In this section, we'll explore real-life case studies and success stories of resellers who have achieved remarkable success in the industry. These stories serve as inspiration and provide valuable insights into the strategies and tactics that have contributed to their success.

Case Study 1:

From Garage Startup to Million-Dollar Business

John Doe's journey from a humble garage startup to a thriving million-dollar business serves as a testament to the power of determination and entrepreneurship. When John started his reselling venture, he faced numerous challenges, including limited funds and fierce competition. However, he refused to be deterred and instead focused on leveraging his strengths and seizing opportunities.

Insights:

- John's success underscores the importance of perseverance and resilience in the face of adversity. Despite facing setbacks and obstacles, he remained committed to his vision and worked tirelessly to achieve his goals.

- By starting small and gradually scaling up his business, John was able to minimize risks and build a solid foundation for growth. He reinvested profits into his business, expanded his product offerings, and invested in marketing and branding efforts to attract customers.

- John's ability to adapt to changing market dynamics and embrace new technologies played a crucial role in his success. He leveraged automation tools and digital platforms to streamline operations, optimize workflows, and enhance customer experiences.

Case Study 2:

<u>**Niche Domination in a Competitive Market**</u>

Jane Smith's story exemplifies the power of niche marketing and customer-centric strategies in a competitive market. Instead of trying to compete with larger resellers on price or volume, Jane focused on carving out a niche for herself by specializing in a specific product category.

<u>Insights:</u>

- Jane's success highlights the importance of identifying a target audience and catering to their unique needs and preferences. By focusing on a niche market, she was able to differentiate herself from competitors and build a loyal customer base.

- Jane's emphasis on quality and customer service set her apart in a crowded marketplace. She sourced high-quality products, provided detailed product descriptions, and offered personalized customer support to ensure customer satisfaction and loyalty.

- Jane's commitment to continuous improvement and innovation enabled her to stay ahead of the competition. She regularly monitored market trends, sought customer feedback, and adapted her strategies to meet evolving consumer demands.

Case Study 3:

Scaling Up with Automation and Technology

Mike Johnson's journey showcases the transformative impact of technology and automation on business growth and scalability. As Mike's reselling business expanded, he recognized the need to streamline operations and optimize efficiency to meet growing demand.

Insights:

- Mike's success underscores the importance of embracing technology as a catalyst for growth and innovation. By leveraging automation tools and software solutions, he was able to automate repetitive tasks, reduce manual errors, and improve operational efficiency.

- Mike's strategic use of data and analytics enabled him to make informed business decisions and identify opportunities for optimization and improvement. He analyzed sales data, inventory levels, and customer behavior to identify trends and patterns and adjust his strategies accordingly.

- Mike's commitment to excellence and customer satisfaction fueled his success. He prioritized transparency, communication, and responsiveness in his interactions with customers and suppliers, building trust and credibility in the marketplace.

Case Study 4:

Overcoming Adversity and Achieving Success

Sarah Lee's story is a testament to the resilience and determination of entrepreneurs in the face of adversity. Despite facing personal challenges and setbacks, Sarah refused to let her circumstances define her and instead used them as fuel to propel her towards success.

Insights:

- Sarah's journey illustrates the power of perseverance and grit in overcoming obstacles and achieving one's goals. Despite facing numerous challenges, she remained focused on her vision and worked tirelessly to turn her dreams into reality.

- Sarah's ability to adapt to adversity and pivot when necessary was key to her success. She embraced change, learned from her failures, and used setbacks as opportunities for growth and self-improvement.

- Sarah's unwavering commitment to her values and principles guided her through difficult times and served as a beacon of inspiration for others. She remained true to herself, maintained integrity in her dealings, and treated others with kindness and respect, earning the admiration and loyalty of her customers and peers.

6.2 Lessons Learned and Best Practices

In this section, we'll distill the key lessons learned from the case studies and highlight best practices that aspiring resellers can apply to their own businesses:

Lesson 1: Find Your Niche

Identifying a niche market or product category is crucial for resellers looking to differentiate themselves and stand out in a crowded marketplace. Instead of trying to appeal to everyone, successful resellers focus on serving a specific segment of customers with unique needs and preferences.

Insights:

- **Market Research:** Conduct thorough market research to identify potential niche markets or product categories that are underserved or have less competition. Look for areas where you can leverage your expertise, interests, or passion to offer something valuable and unique to customers.

- **Target Audience:** Understand the demographics, behaviors, and preferences of your target audience within your chosen niche. Tailor your product offerings, marketing messages, and customer experiences to resonate with their needs and interests.

- **Competitive Analysis:** Analyze your competitors operating within the same niche to identify gaps, opportunities, and areas where you can differentiate yourself. Determine what sets you apart from competitors and how you can leverage your strengths to position yourself as a leader in your niche.

Lesson 2: Prioritize Quality

In the competitive world of reselling, quality should always be a top priority. Investing in high-quality products, providing accurate product descriptions, and offering exceptional customer service are essential for building trust and loyalty with your audience.

Insights:

- **Product Sourcing:** Source products from reputable suppliers and manufacturers known for producing high-quality goods. Conduct thorough inspections and quality checks to ensure that the products meet your standards before offering them to customers.

- **Accurate Descriptions:** Provide detailed and accurate product descriptions that clearly communicate the features, specifications, and benefits of each item. Include high-quality images and videos to give customers a clear understanding of what they can expect.

- **Exceptional Service:** Offer exceptional customer service at every touchpoint of the buying journey. Be responsive to customer inquiries, address concerns promptly, and go above and beyond to exceed customer expectations. Building strong relationships with your customers can lead to repeat business and positive word-of-mouth referrals.

Lesson 3: Embrace Technology

Technology can be a game-changer for resellers, enabling them to streamline operations, optimize efficiency, and enhance the customer experience. Leveraging automation tools, software solutions, and digital platforms can help resellers stay competitive in today's fast-paced marketplace.

Insights:

- **Automation:** Automate repetitive tasks such as inventory management, order processing, and customer communication to save time and reduce manual errors. Invest in inventory management software, customer relationship management (CRM) systems, and email marketing automation tools to streamline workflows and improve productivity.

- **Data Analysis:** Harness the power of data and analytics to gain insights into customer behavior, market trends, and business performance. Analyze sales data, customer feedback, and website metrics to identify opportunities for optimization and improvement. Use data-driven insights to make informed business decisions and drive growth.

- **Digital Platforms:** Leverage digital platforms such as e-commerce websites, social media channels, and online marketplaces to reach a wider audience and expand your market reach. Invest in search engine optimization (SEO), pay-per-click (PPC) advertising, and social media marketing to drive traffic and generate sales online.

Lesson 4: Adapt and Innovate

The business landscape is constantly evolving, and successful resellers must be willing to adapt to changing market conditions and consumer preferences. Staying flexible, open-minded, and proactive in identifying new opportunities and adapting strategies accordingly is key to long-term success.

Insights:

- **Market Monitoring:** Stay informed about market trends, competitor activities, and emerging technologies that could impact your business. Monitor changes in consumer behavior, preferences, and purchasing patterns to anticipate shifts in demand and adapt your strategies accordingly.

- **Agility:** Maintain agility and flexibility in your business operations to respond quickly to changing market dynamics. Be willing to pivot and experiment with new ideas, products, or marketing strategies to stay ahead of the competition and capitalize on emerging opportunities.

- **Innovation:** Foster a culture of innovation and creativity within your organization to drive continuous improvement and stay ahead of the curve. Encourage employees to think outside the box, experiment with new approaches, and embrace change as a catalyst for growth and innovation.

6.3 Inspirational Stories for Motivation

In this final section, we'll share inspirational stories and anecdotes from successful resellers to motivate and inspire readers on their entrepreneurial journey. These stories highlight the resilience, determination, and passion of individuals who have overcome obstacles and achieved their goals through hard work and perseverance.

Story 1: The Power of Persistence

Meet Mark, a reseller who embarked on his entrepreneurial journey with a passion for turning thrift store finds into profitable ventures. Despite facing initial setbacks and financial constraints, Mark's unwavering determination fueled his persistence. He spent countless hours scouring thrift stores, flea markets, and garage sales for hidden gems to resell online.

Mark encountered challenges along the way, including inventory shortages, shipping delays, and fluctuating market demand. However, he refused to be discouraged by temporary setbacks and instead viewed them as opportunities for growth and learning. Through perseverance and adaptability, Mark honed his sourcing skills, optimized his selling strategies, and steadily grew his reselling business.

After years of hard work and dedication, Mark's persistence paid off as his business flourished. He expanded his product offerings, diversified his sales channels, and built a loyal customer base. Today, Mark's reselling business generates steady revenue and provides him with the flexibility and freedom to pursue his passions and live life on his own terms.

Story 2: Turning Adversity into Opportunity

Sarah's journey to entrepreneurship began with a sudden job loss and financial hardship. Faced with uncertainty and adversity, Sarah decided to take control of her destiny by starting her own reselling business. Armed with determination and resourcefulness, Sarah embarked on a journey of self-discovery and transformation.

Despite limited resources and minimal experience in the reselling industry, Sarah refused to let fear hold her back. She embraced challenges as opportunities for growth and innovation, leveraging her creativity and ingenuity to source unique products and connect with customers. Through trial and error, Sarah learned valuable lessons about resilience, adaptability, and perseverance.

As her reselling business grew, Sarah's confidence and resilience blossomed. She embraced her role as an entrepreneur, empowering herself and inspiring others with her courage and tenacity. Today, Sarah's reselling business serves as a testament to the power of resilience and the potential for growth and success, even in the face of adversity.

Story 3: The Journey of Self-Discovery

John's journey to entrepreneurship was a path of self-discovery and personal growth. Dissatisfied with his corporate job and longing for fulfillment, John embarked on a journey to find his true calling. Inspired by his passion for entrepreneurship and a desire for autonomy, John took a leap of faith and started his own reselling business.

Along the way, John discovered his strengths, interests, and values, and aligned them with his entrepreneurial pursuits. He embraced challenges as opportunities for self-improvement and growth, honing his skills in sourcing, marketing, and customer service. Through perseverance and introspection, John found fulfillment and purpose in building a business that reflected his passions and aspirations.

Today, John's reselling business not only provides him with financial stability but also offers him a sense of fulfillment and satisfaction. By embracing his journey of self-discovery, John has unlocked his true potential and found joy and fulfillment in pursuing his entrepreneurial dreams.

Story 4: Empowering Others Through Success

Jane's entrepreneurial journey was fueled by a desire to make a positive impact in her community and empower others. After achieving success in her reselling business, Jane felt a calling to give back and pay it forward. She recognized the importance of using her platform for social good and sought opportunities to uplift and inspire others.

Jane became actively involved in mentoring aspiring entrepreneurs, sharing her knowledge and expertise to help them navigate the challenges of starting and growing a business. She volunteered her time and resources to support charitable causes and community initiatives, using her business success as a platform for philanthropy and social responsibility.

Through her acts of kindness and generosity, Jane inspired others to believe in themselves and pursue their dreams. She demonstrated that success is not just about financial gains but also about making a positive impact and leaving a lasting legacy. Jane's commitment to empowering others through success serves as a beacon of hope and inspiration for aspiring entrepreneurs around the world.

CHAPTER 7:

Where to Buy Amazon Return Pallets in the UK

In this chapter, we'll explore the various sources and platforms where resellers can purchase Amazon return pallets in the UK. From online marketplaces to liquidation auctions, we'll cover the options available to resellers looking to source inventory for their businesses.

- ## Online Marketplaces

Online marketplaces such as B-Stock, Wholesale Clearance UK, and Wholesale Deals offer a wide selection of Amazon return pallets for sale. We'll discuss how to navigate these platforms, find reputable sellers, and bid on pallets that meet your sourcing criteria.

- ## Liquidation Auctions

Liquidation auctions are another option for purchasing Amazon return pallets in the UK. Companies like John Pye Auctions and All Stars Wholesale offer regular auctions featuring a variety of pallets, including Amazon returns. We'll discuss how to participate in these auctions and maximize your chances of winning pallets at competitive prices.

- ## Wholesale Suppliers

Some wholesale suppliers specialize in offering Amazon return pallets directly to resellers. We'll explore how to find and vet wholesale suppliers, negotiate pricing and terms, and establish long-term relationships to ensure a consistent supply of inventory for your business.

- ## Trade Shows and Expos

Trade shows and expos provide opportunities for resellers to connect with suppliers and explore new sourcing options. We'll discuss upcoming events in the UK where resellers can network with industry professionals, attend seminars, and discover new products and suppliers.

- ## Local Auction Houses

Local auction houses may also offer Amazon return pallets for sale, either through live auctions or online bidding platforms. We'll explore how to find and participate in local auctions, as well as tips for evaluating pallets and determining their potential profitability.

- ## Networking Groups and Forums

Networking groups and online forums can be valuable resources for connecting with other resellers and sharing sourcing tips and recommendations. We'll discuss popular networking groups and forums in the UK where resellers can exchange information, ask questions, and learn from each other's experiences.

CHAPTER 8:

Where to Buy Amazon Return Pallets in Canada

In this chapter, we'll explore the various sources and platforms where resellers can purchase Amazon return pallets in Canada. From online marketplaces to liquidation auctions, we'll cover the options available to resellers looking to source inventory for their businesses north of the border.

- ## Online Marketplaces

Online marketplaces such as Direct Liquidation, Quicklotz, and BULQ offer a wide selection of Amazon return pallets for sale in Canada. We'll discuss how to navigate these platforms, find reputable sellers, and bid on pallets that meet your sourcing criteria while taking into account Canadian regulations and shipping considerations.

- ## Liquidation Auctions

Liquidation auctions are another viable option for purchasing Amazon return pallets in Canada. Companies like B-Stock

Solutions and 888 Lots host regular auctions featuring a variety of pallets, including Amazon returns. We'll discuss how to participate in these auctions and maximize your chances of winning pallets at competitive prices, considering factors like shipping costs and customs clearance.

- ## Wholesale Suppliers

Some wholesale suppliers specialize in offering Amazon return pallets directly to resellers in Canada. We'll explore how to find and vet these suppliers, negotiate pricing and terms, and establish reliable partnerships to ensure a steady supply of inventory for your business while navigating Canadian regulations and import/export laws.

- ## Trade Shows and Expos

Trade shows and expos provide valuable opportunities for resellers to connect with suppliers and explore new sourcing options in Canada. We'll discuss upcoming events across the country where resellers can network with industry professionals, attend seminars, and discover new products and suppliers relevant to the Canadian market.

- ## Local Auction Houses

Local auction houses may also offer Amazon return pallets for sale in Canada, either through live auctions or online bidding platforms. We'll explore how to find and participate in these auctions, as well as tips for evaluating pallets and assessing their potential profitability while considering local regulations and tax implications.

- ## Networking Groups and Forums

Networking groups and online forums serve as valuable resources for Canadian resellers to connect with peers, share sourcing strategies, and exchange insights. We'll discuss popular networking groups and forums where resellers can engage with the community, seek advice, and stay informed about the latest trends and opportunities in the Canadian reselling market.

CONCLUSION

In this final chapter, we'll delve deeper into the key insights and takeaways from our exploration of buying and selling Amazon return pallets. We'll reflect on the transformative journey that readers have embarked on throughout this book, offering practical guidance and heartfelt encouragement to empower them in their reselling endeavors.

• Recap of Key Insights

As we conclude our journey together, it's essential to revisit the foundational principles and actionable strategies that have been discussed in earlier chapters. From understanding the intricacies of Amazon return pallets to mastering sourcing strategies and sales tactics, readers have gained a wealth of knowledge to guide them on their reselling journey.

We'll provide a comprehensive recap of the main topics covered, highlighting key insights and best practices that readers can implement in their own businesses. This recap serves as a valuable reference point, reinforcing essential concepts and ensuring that readers are well-equipped to navigate the complexities of the reselling landscape.

- ## Reflection and Self-Assessment

Encouraging readers to engage in introspection and self-assessment, we'll invite them to reflect on their individual strengths, weaknesses, and areas for growth. By taking stock of their skills, experiences, and aspirations, readers can gain valuable insights into where they stand on their entrepreneurial journey and identify opportunities for personal and professional development.

We'll provide guiding questions and prompts to facilitate this reflection process, encouraging readers to consider their goals, values, and motivations. Through self-awareness and introspection, readers can gain clarity on their priorities and chart a course towards success that aligns with their unique strengths and aspirations.

- ## Setting Goals and Taking Action

Setting goals is a critical step in the journey towards success, and we'll guide readers through the process of defining clear and achievable objectives for their reselling businesses. Whether it's increasing sales revenue, expanding their product line, or enhancing customer satisfaction, setting specific, measurable, and actionable goals is essential for driving progress and maintaining momentum.

We'll provide practical tips and strategies for setting SMART goals—goals that are Specific, Measurable, Achievable, Relevant, and Time-bound. By breaking down larger objectives into smaller, manageable tasks, readers can create a roadmap for success and take concrete steps towards realizing their vision for their reselling business.

- ## Embracing the Journey

Entrepreneurship is a journey filled with challenges, triumphs, and unexpected twists and turns. In this section, we'll explore the importance of embracing the journey and cultivating a mindset of resilience, adaptability, and perseverance.

We'll share stories of resilience and perseverance from successful entrepreneurs who have overcome obstacles and setbacks on their path to success. These stories serve as inspiration for readers, demonstrating that setbacks are not roadblocks but opportunities for growth and learning.

We'll provide practical strategies for overcoming common challenges faced by resellers, such as inventory shortages, pricing pressure, and competitive threats. From leveraging technology to streamlining operations, readers will learn how to navigate obstacles with confidence and determination.

- ## Continuing Education and Growth

In the ever-evolving world of reselling, lifelong learning is essential for staying competitive and innovative. In this section, we'll explore opportunities for continuing education and professional development, from online courses and workshops to industry conferences and networking events.

We'll highlight resources and organizations that offer valuable insights and expertise in the reselling industry, empowering readers to expand their knowledge, hone their skills, and stay ahead of the curve. By investing in their personal and professional growth, readers can position themselves for long-term success and sustainability in the reselling market.

Expressing Gratitude

As we bid farewell to our readers, we want to express our deepest gratitude for joining us on this reselling journey. Your commitment to learning and growth has been truly inspiring, and we are honored to have been a part of your entrepreneurial endeavors.

We extend our heartfelt thanks to our readers for their support, engagement, and enthusiasm throughout this book. Your feedback and contributions have enriched our discussion and fueled our passion for empowering resellers around the world.

Final Words of Encouragement

In closing, we want to leave our readers with a final message of encouragement and empowerment. As you continue on your reselling journey, remember that success is not defined by the destination but by the journey itself. Embrace the challenges, celebrate the victories, and never lose sight of your vision for a thriving and fulfilling reselling business.

We believe in your potential to achieve greatness in the reselling industry, and we're excited to see where your entrepreneurial journey takes you. Remember to stay resilient, stay focused, and stay passionate about your goals, knowing that with dedication and determination, anything is possible.

A GLOSSARY OF RESELLING TERMS

This comprehensive glossary serves as a valuable reference tool for readers, providing detailed definitions and explanations of key terms and concepts commonly used in the reselling industry. From terminology related to sourcing and inventory management to sales strategies and marketing techniques, readers can refer to this appendix to enhance their understanding and proficiency in the world of reselling.

The glossary covers a wide range of topics, including:

- **Sourcing:** Definitions of terms related to sourcing products, such as wholesale, liquidation, and arbitrage.

- **Inventory Management:** Explanations of inventory management concepts, including SKU, turnover rate, and stock keeping unit.

- **Sales and Marketing**: Definitions of sales and marketing terms, such as cross-selling, upselling, and conversion rate optimization.

- **E-commerce Platforms**: Explanations of terms associated with online marketplaces and platforms, such as FBA (Fulfillment by Amazon), eBay, and Shopify.

- **Financial Terms**: Definitions of financial terms relevant to reselling, including gross profit, net profit, and return on investment (ROI).

- **Legal and Compliance:** Explanations of legal and compliance terms, such as liability, copyright, and terms of service.

Readers can use this glossary as a comprehensive resource to clarify any unfamiliar terms encountered throughout their reselling journey, ensuring they have a solid understanding of the terminology used in the industry.

RECOMMENDED RESOURCES AND TOOLS

In this appendix, we provide readers with a curated list of recommended resources and tools to support them in their reselling endeavors. From software applications and online platforms to educational resources and professional associations, readers will find a diverse range of resources to help them succeed in the reselling industry.

The appendix includes:

- **Inventory Management Software:** Recommendations for software applications designed to streamline inventory management processes, track sales, and analyze performance metrics.

- **Pricing Tools**: Suggestions for tools and resources to assist resellers in pricing their products competitively and maximizing profitability.

- **Online Marketplaces**: Recommendations for popular online marketplaces and platforms where resellers can source and sell products, such as Amazon, eBay, and Walmart Marketplace.

- **Industry Associations**: Information about professional associations and organizations dedicated to supporting resellers and providing networking opportunities, educational resources, and advocacy.

- **Educational Resources**: Suggestions for books, courses, workshops, and online tutorials to help resellers enhance their skills, expand their knowledge, and stay updated on industry trends.

- **Community Forums and Groups**: Recommendations for online forums, social media groups, and networking communities where resellers can connect with peers, share insights, and seek advice.

By leveraging these recommended resources and tools, readers can streamline their operations, optimize their strategies, and stay informed about the latest developments in the reselling industry.

ADDITIONAL READING SUGGESTIONS

For readers eager to deepen their understanding of reselling and entrepreneurship, this appendix offers a curated list of additional reading suggestions. From books and articles to podcasts and online courses, readers will find a wealth of resources to further their learning and professional development in the reselling industry.

The appendix includes recommendations for:

- Books: Suggestions for books covering a wide range of topics related to reselling, entrepreneurship, business management, and personal development.

- Articles and Blog Posts: Recommendations for online articles, blog posts, and industry publications offering insights, tips, and analysis relevant to reselling and business ownership.

- Podcasts: Suggestions for podcasts featuring interviews, discussions, and expert insights on reselling, e-commerce, and entrepreneurship.

- Online Courses: Recommendations for online courses and educational platforms offering specialized training in reselling, marketing, finance, and other relevant topics.

By exploring these additional reading suggestions, readers can expand their knowledge, gain new perspectives, and continue their journey of professional growth and development in the reselling industry.

Made in the USA
Las Vegas, NV
26 December 2024